PLAY

WORK AT PLAY OR PLAY AT WORK

BRADLEY CHARBONNEAU

REPOSSIBLE

Copyright © 2021 by Bradley Charbonneau

All rights reserved.

No part of this book may be reproduced in any form or by any electronic or mechanical means, including information storage and retrieval systems, without written permission from the author, except for the use of brief quotations in a book review.

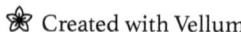 Created with Vellum

PREFACE

Want to join us in building, growing, and molding what this book will become?

Or maybe even just watch a video of each letter of P.L.A.Y. that might turn into:

1. Permit
2. Leap
3. Anchor
4. Yield

Come join us for "more than words on a page" over at play.repossible.com.

We'll be sharing direct links to specific chapter-related media and if you're already set up with a (free) account, it will be all the more seamless.

See you there!

"Work consists of whatever a body is obliged to do. Play consists of whatever a body is not obliged to do."

— MARK TWAIN, FROM "THE ADVENTURES OF TOM SAWYER"

DEDICATION

For Mom

*Who taught me that, although work was important, play was exponentially more important and, if you did it right, could complete the circle and turn **work** into **play.***

CONTENTS

Introduction   xi

Prologue   1
Foreword   7

PART I
P | PERMIT

1. Plant   11
2. Parade   16
3. Plunge   21
4. Plastic   24
5. Prepare   26
6. Practice   31

PART II
L | LEAP

7. Loosen   35
8. Lose   37
9. Laugh   39
10. Leonard   41
11. Louise   44

PART III
A | ANCHOR

12. Anchor   49
13. Adwynna   51

PART IV
Y | YIELD

14. Yell   57
15. Yodel   60
16. Yield   62

Afterword   65
Epilogue   67

Acknowledgments	69
About the Author	71
Also by Bradley Charbonneau	75
The End	78

INTRODUCTION
REPOSSIBLE

Welcome to Play!

However, a warning, a disclaimer, a note from the (lack of) management here at Repossible.

This is book number ten in the Repossible series. We're deep into it by now.

The Repossible Series

1. Repossible
2. Every Single Day
3. Ask
4. Dare
5. Create
6. Decide
7. Meditate
8. Spark
9. Surrender
10. **Play**
11. Celebrate

12. Evaluate
13. Elevate
14. Share

The series ascends from the harder, more "grounded" ideas of:

1. Ask
2. Dare
3. Decide
4. etc.

to the lighter, more fun, easier and even "out there" concepts of:

1. Meditate
2. Surrender
3. Play
4. Celebrate
5. etc.

If the earlier books are the grounded roots and the trunk of the tree, then the later books are the branches and the leaves.

Those leaves wouldn't exist without the roots.

But the roots also need the leaves.

If earlier on, it can mean making big decisions and forcing actions and it's hard and not fun and seems like a waste of time, then later on it can seem even too easy, way too much fun, and we realize that earlier on was not a waste of time at all.

It's a process, a roadmap.

Some of us (not me!) might jump into the level of play without missing a beat. Lucky them!

Most of us need to take the steps to get here.

This book is about achieving a level of "enlightenment" that might seem unattainable to some yet I believe it's reachable for all of us in some way, shape, or form.

If you're not "ready" for this book yet and you need to *create* more or *meditate* more, then by all means, put this down when you need to and come back to it later.

If you need to *ask* the big questions or *dare* to answer them. Maybe you need to *decide* what you're going to do next or develop a *meditation* practice, go do all of that first.

At some point, the idea of *play* is going to feel right but if it's not time yet then it's not time yet.

There you have it.

If you're ready to turn the page and begin down a path of lightness, happiness, and profound joy, here we go.

PROLOGUE
ENLIGHTENMENT

Do people use dictionaries much anymore? I know I don't use them much (D'oh! Says the writer! Blasphemy!) but when I'm digging deep, like writing a book, it's one of those things you do when afterwards you say, "Gee, why don't I do this more often?"

Here are some definitions for the verb.

Play

- to exercise or employ oneself in diversion, **amusement**, or recreation
- to take part or engage in a **game**
- to take part in a game for stakes; **gamble**
- to **act** on or as if on the stage; **perform**
- to move about **lightly** or quickly

In choosing just the right verb for each book in the Repossible series, I come across other top contenders. One of them for this book was: **enlighten**. Although the verb doesn't quite get to the noun I'm shooting for: **enlightenment**.

Back to the dictionary:

Enlightenment

- Buddhism : a final blessed state marked by the absence of desire or suffering

There are other definitions, most referring to "the state of being enlightened" so let's go there.

Enlightened

- freed from ignorance and misinformation
- based on full comprehension of the problems involved

Are you feeling where I'm heading?

Although I kept the **play** title for the "childlike" and the "innocence" of it and also because enlightenment is going to get me in trouble with my guru buddies on hilltops in Nepal, I see "play" as a state of mind, almost a (spiritual?) place where you go or live, or a mindset that you embrace or even a mantra you live by.

Check out that Buddhist bit there again: a "blessed state marked by **absence of desire or suffering.**"

Absence of desire? Whoa, really?

OK, I get the absence of suffering because, you know, suffering sounds terrible and all, but absence of desire?

Interesting, right?

Yet this is where we're heading.

We reach a level of enlightenment or of play when we no longer desire.

We could see this a few ways.

1. I *have* everything I want (thus, absence of desire)
2. I *am* everything I want (thus, absence of desire)

You can probably guess where I'm going to with this. "Have" gets us most often to stuff and things and cars and, I don't know, houses.

But "am"? Can you say this out loud?

"I am everything I want."

I'm going to go out on a limb and say "absence of desire" might be a little drastic, a bit harsh, even going too far.

That would be, in my humble opinion, like the often misinterpreted idea that meditation is to reach "absence of all thought."

You know what? It's just not possible. Well, unless you're a Nepalese monk or dead. But even more important, I don't think it's the goal (absence of thought or even absence of desire).

I'm going to toss a bit of my born-in-California in here and put it this way:

"I have desire but I'm good. I got this."

Play. Enlightenment. (Absence of) desire.

How are we doing?

I know, we're only in the Prologue of this book and we're digging deep. Just wait until the Parade chapter when I really let loose about what Play is *not*.

Yet the stubborn "nutty professor" in me disregards all good book promotion tactics, defies author marketing strategies, and keeps giving my books titles that I know will, eventually, hit home, sink in, and *resonate*.

Some author with "better" marketing skills than I have might have called this book:

- 17 fail-proof tactics to reach spiritual, emotional, and financial enlightenment

- How to achieve true happiness, become the person you always wanted to be, while keeping a smile on your face and making your friends wonder what drug you're taking
- Take your meditation practice to the next level and join the elite ranks of enlightened Nepalese monks without getting on a plane or donning an orange robe

OK, yeah, sorry about that.

A friend of mine, who's been through a bit of a rough patch in recent months, told me:

 "I'm going to start taking this a lot more seriously."

— Well-meaning friend

Although I completely understood what he meant, I felt the need to at least suggest one little tweak to his plans for the future.

I suggested he change one little word in there so that his future life would become more, well, enlightened, happy, fulfilled, overflowing with meaning, deep laughs, broad smiles, and a gratefulness previously unknown.

I thought he might reword it like this:

 "I'm going to start taking this a lot less seriously."

— Same friend (probably after having read this prologue...)

We're about done here.

Play is the title. Enlightenment, or whatever definition or word you're striving for, is where we're heading.

I'm not changing the title.

Because, according to Mark Twain, play consists of what a body is not obliged to do but I would add that it's something we want to do, we are thankful to be able to do, and that we will continue to do from here on out.

Until we die.
And truly become enlightened.

- **Possible:** visit Nepal
- **Impossible:** enlightenment
- **Repossible:** play

FOREWORD
BY S. KEPTIC

I'm skeptical.

Seriously, a book called "Play"? For adults?

I mean, sure, for kids, I get it. They need to learn how to play just like they need to learn how to obey their parents, do their chores, and learn how to manage their allowance.

But adults?

Haven't we outgrown this notion?

C'mon, here's all you need:

1. Work hard
2. Keep your head down
3. Carry on

There's no magic, no secret, no "book" that's going to sway me from the serious, professional, successful individual I am into becoming, what? A kid? Some kind of laughing clown, a stand-up comedian?

That's just not who I am.

Mr. Charbonneau says that in a state of Play, we can reach higher levels of clarity and combine those with less hard work to achieve results we haven't even imagined yet.

How am I supposed to achieve something I haven't even imagined yet?

I'm just going to work hard, keep my head down, and carry on.

"Play!"

As if!

You go ahead and read this book and if it works for you, good for you.

If not, I'll see you in long line outside of of the rerun hit film, "Life Goes On."

S. Keptic
Ph.D. in Serious Studies
Old Somewhere
November 2020

PART I
P | PERMIT

1

PLANT

THE DEEPER THE ROOTS, THE HIGHER THE BRANCHES

 "The deeper the roots, the higher the branches."

— BRADLEY CHARBONNEAU

Author's Note: I try to find quotes for each chapter as I like to get a third-party perspective or wording or angle on the topic of the chapter.

But this was the quote I was looking for:

"The deeper the roots, the higher the branches."

All I could find was a website post about tree symbolism with the title with the quote I wanted but then went on about:

> "Yggdrasil unites the multiple worlds of Norse myth into a single entity..."

Which I didn't really understand.

If you can find someone who said what I want to say, please let me know. Otherwise, here we go.

Because this chapter is often overlooked—and it's kind of crazy important.

Here we are in the Play book. It's all about rising up, lifting, soaring above the trees. We're up there playing, dare I say frolicking, and life is good, easy, and we might have a ball to throw around or a drink with an umbrella in it but the wind is in our hair and we're smiling.

Yep, things are good up there at the top of the tree. That is one view I have on the concept of Play.

Yet let's have a look at that tall tree.

What's holding it into the ground below? What's keeping it from toppling over in a storm? How deep are the roots firmly planted in the soil? What kind of soil is it: sand, granite?

If we're up there, playing ball with friends and spilling frilly drinks, what's keeping the tree from:

1. Completely floating away
2. Falling over
3. Getting top heavy and bending over like a gymnast

Let's dig into a few "definitions" although not from the dictionary but to lay the groundwork as to what we mean with Play and how we're going to get there and yet keep the roots deep so we don't topple over.

Roots (Ask, Create, "Work")

Remember way back in Ask? Wow, that was a long time ago: both book-wise, number of pages, but also along our transformational adventure. We asked the tough questions such as:

1. Who will we become next?
2. What do we truly and deeply "want" from life?
3. Where have we been—and how can it help us get to where we're going?
4. Do you put pepper spray on your burrito?

5. Where are we now?
6. What tiny, daily actions do we need to do to get from where we are to where we want to go?

Whew! It's the real stuff. It's the hard stuff. Here we are in the book Play talking about light and fun and smiles and yet here I am bringing back the dredge from the sludge of the cellar where we ask the tough questions.

Yep.

Those are the roots.

The foundation from which we grow, rise up, and go forward.

Here's something to keep in mind: that tree? The trunk, the thicker branches down below? None of it would exist without the roots.

Yep, later on, the branches are where the fun stuff happens but we are thankful for those roots as they allowed us to get way up top here.

The roots are also our daily habits, our Every Single Day, Create, and our Decide.

They are usually less fun or playful but they are also necessary.

Silly analogy? You brush your teeth every single day (roots) and then you notice your sparkly, pearly whites and feel a sense of pride and beauty (branches).

Although, one caveat, whereas many people think of brushing their teeth as a chore, I actually like it. But hey, I also think "working" on a book is fun on a Sunday morning before the rest of my family is up and my dog is at my feet and THIS is both my roots and my branches.

Oops, did you catch that?

I let that slip.

The roots can become the branches.

What you think you "must" do can also become what you're "allowed" to do.

I'm rising up to the branches. Let's get to that section of this chapter.

Branches (Play)

I'm going to borrow from the epigraph of this book.

> "**Work** consists of whatever a body is obliged to do. **Play** consists of whatever a body is not obliged to do."
>
> — Mark Twain

There are people who work super hard, maybe have done so their whole lives, and if, oh, I don't know, they're interviewed about winning the lottery and they answer with what they would do with the winnings, it often goes something along the lines of:

> "I would buy a yacht and sail around the Caribbean sipping Mai Tais all day and do absolutely nothing and enjoy every single minute of it."
>
> — Probably Not Lottery Winner

I believe them. Well, I believe that this is their dream.

At least in part because their current life, according to the esteemed Mr. Mark Twain, is probably too much "work" and not enough "play." Too much of what they're obliged to do and not enough about what they're not obliged to do.

Too much "work" and not enough "play."

As I mentioned at the end of the section above called Roots (Ask, Create, "Work"), the goal, or at least my goal, is to **turn what most think of as work, as the obligational task, into the play thing, the optional thing, the thing we feel lucky to be able to do.**

For me, it's writing to you here on a Sunday morning.

What is it for you?

- **Possible:** fly higher

- **Impossible:** never land
- **Repossible:** dig deeper

2

PARADE

YOU CAN'T JOIN THE PARADE IF YOU DIDN'T WIN THE CHAMPIONSHIP

 "You can't buy a good reputation; you must earn it."

— Harvey Mackay

You're going to ask me how I know this but let's just say I know from experience.

There are going to be times in this book when you say something along the lines of:

 "Dude. Like, no way."

— Surfer Reader

Each of us is going to have his or her own definitions, ideas, and visions of what Play means to us.

Let's go back to the parade for a moment. Let's make it a boat parade. In a harbor.

I saw this recently so it's fresh.

We were in Ouderkerk aan de Amstel (a ridiculously quaint little town outside of Amsterdam) when I saw a guy who could have been the cover photo for this book. This book called Play.

If you read the Prologue where we talked about big ideas like enlightenment, you might begin to have an idea of the scene.

A man, maybe 56 years old, salt and pepper hair with just the right mix of sailor and wind-whipped, white button-down shirt, shorts that fit, tan, and the cocktail glass in hand.

Can you see him?

He's in his sleek yet traditional boat with a collection of his closest friends. He's known them for years. He's comfortable with them—and them with him.

He's at home, he's at ease, he's in charge.

He's happy, content, even joyful.

Yet.

But.

Wait.

Here's where I want to, early on in this book, make something clear.

This gentleman, Mr. Sailor Captain, exudes the air of someone whom I am describing here as having the Play mindset yet I think I know what you're thinking.

Might I take a guess?

You're thinking:

 "Yeah, of course he's at Play, Mr. Charbonneau, he's wealthy!"

"Maybe it's a rental boat and it's all a facade to show off to his friends."

"How do we know he has truly ascended to the level of Play, on which this book is based? Maybe he's just having a fun day and he's deep in debt, his wife ran off with the mailman, and he's miserable?"

— Maybe You

This is one of those moments, as an author, when I'm working here to get across an idea, a vision even, of something I have in my mind and I'm doing my best to share that with you so that we can see and experience the same things or at least similarly.

Nope, you're right. We don't know much else about Captain Happy. On the surface, he sure looks happy.

Maybe he won the lottery last week and bought this boat and some new shorts and my perspective on him is based only on his nice boat and shiny cocktail glass?

Yep. Maybe.

I'm going to copy and paste the quote from the beginning of this chapter again here.

 "You can't buy a good reputation; you must earn it."

— Harvey Mackay

I would change it up, for the purposes of this book title Play, to make it:

 "You can't buy the Play mindset; you must earn it."

— Bradley Charbonneau

So maybe Mr. True Sailor has earned it and he's living the Play lifestyle.

Maybe he won the lottery and he's not quite there yet—or never will be.

Maybe I've got it all wrong.

But I hear you asking:

 "Bradley, where are you going with this?"

— You, reader, asking me, writer

As with each of the books in the Repossible series, we're going to have our own versions of the *character* of the book.

For Meditate, maybe you have that sly cat.

For Spark, you might have a mom and daughter writing a book together.

For Play, we need to strive towards a character, a persona, a type or mindset of a person that we want to become.

Yet, the parade, the title of this chapter, is earned.

Mr. Lottery Winner doesn't get the Play certificate only because he has the money to buy a boat and cocktail glasses.

Maybe Mr. True Sailor does, maybe he doesn't.

In the prologue, when talking about enlightenment, there was mention of suffering. I don't know if we need to know suffering before we can reach a level of Play but I know we need to know a lower level before we can reach a higher level if only to recognize that we have ascended from a place where we were and now acknowledge and respect the level of Play we have achieved.

Finally, it's not the guy sitting in the café on the side of the river who gets to say or distinguish or classify someone as having reached the level of Play or not.

It comes from that person him or herself.

We are usually our harshest critics who bring us down to levels we may or may not deserve yet we must also Celebrate our ascension to the level of Play.

We can watch the parade of Players from the riverbank.

We can celebrate and toast while in the boat in the river.

Yet the true ascension to Play is when you're in the boat and you're not thinking about any of this and you're enjoying your friends, the blue sky, the water lapping on the side of your boat, and you have earned the parade, yet you don't care about the parade, and you are the parade.

You are the parade.

- **Possible:** watch the parade
- **Impossible:** parade (without earning it)
- **Repossible:** earn the parade

3

PLUNGE
EXPLORE

> "We must go beyond textbooks, go out into the bypaths and untrodden depths of the wilderness and travel and explore and tell the world the glories of our journey."
>
> — John Hope Franklin

I'm absolutely a rule breaker and that part of me would have titled this chapter:

Explore

Yet I also am a firm believer in the idea that:

> "Constraint breeds creativity."
>
> — (I can't find who said this.)

I found this:

> "The enemy of art is the absence of limitation."

— Orson Welles

So I use "Plunge" as a way to get to Explore.

Plunge is nice because you really get the feeling that you're jumping in, maybe into a lake where you're not sure what's in there, how deep it is, or if there's that slimy moss on the bottom that's going to get in your toes.

But explore gets us to travel, experience, new, unknown, mystery, discovery and lots more.

When you're feeling down, scared, weak, concerned, you're not in the mood to go exploring or traveling. You want to stay home, sit on the couch and watch Netflix.

But when your spirits are up, you're feeling better, stronger, and more alive, you want to explore, to go beyond what you already know, dare to venture to places you've never been.

Then it's easy. Then we can all do it.

Then this chapter is over.

So let's ratchet up the difficulty level a notch.

Challenge

I'm going to offer a challenge here.

Have you ever felt down or weak or tired and stayed in and slept it off? Of course, we all have.

But what about if you did step out of the house when you're down?

Even when you don't feel like it?

When Bradley Charbonneau's Play book looks like an annoying collection of happy pages that you'd rather eat than read?

Because you don't feel like playing.

But can we?

Can we bridge that void?

Make the leap?

Here comes the answer.

Solution

I wish I could say I was always strong enough to just get up, just put on the shoes, and force my way out the door. Alas.

This is where, more often than not, the third party comes into play. An external factor or environmental player that gets you out the door (or started on the project or taking the first step towards whatever it is you're doing).

For me, it's often Pepper.

He's our dog.

When I'm feeling lethargic, empty of ideas, and just like "tomorrow will be better than today," there's one constant who doesn't care in the slightest how I'm feeling: Pepper.

He just wants to go outside. In fact, he needs to go outside. He needs me to bring him to the woods nearby.

The challenge? Explore when you don't feel like it. Head out the door, start the chapter, hit record, do whatever it is you know you need to do to get going, to move those brain cells (and/or legs!) to put you into action—literally.

I add this challenge because a chapter on exploring when we're feeling great and powerful and brilliant is easy. We all do that.

We need the push—the pull—when we're not at our best.

It's one of my "big secrets" to creativity, productivity, and general deep joy: do it anyway, get out the door, start when you don't feel like it.

And yes, most of the time, Pepper is giving me the look that triggers my action.

Speaking of which, he's looking at me right this second.

What—or who—is your trigger to get you to explore? To take the plunge? To go and play even when you're not feeling up to it.

- **Possible:** just make the chapter title "Explore"
- **Impossible:** make "explore" begin with a "P"
- **Repossible:** explore forward and don't look back

4

PLASTIC
GOLD AND RICHES AND GLITTERY GLORY? UH, NO.

> "A child who does not play is not a child, but the man who doesn't play has lost forever the child who lived in him and who he will miss terribly."
>
> — Pablo Neruda

Wait a minute. Those are little bubbles of gold. That's an ocean of playful.
  Colorful plastic? Yep.

SOURCE: It's early Saturday morning as I write this. I'm just out of a powerful meditation where, as we were onto the third "region" of focus, I opened up to "whatever may come." It's an important part of Meditation, the Surrender. At first glance, I was laying in a bath of tiny balls of gold. Glittery and yummy, delicious and rich. I was, quite literally, floating in wealth. Yet, the scene morphed (as it tends to do in meditation) and it was no longer gold and glittery but colorful and ... plastic. I was now in one of those play pens of colorful plastic balls that 7-year-olds somehow find fascinating.

— STRAIGHT FROM SOURCE

As I had "asked" for the unknown, for whatever may come, and, maybe not-so-subconsciously, based on ego, and lower-level desires, I wanted wealth, money, and it came, briefly, in the form of a bath of gold spheres.

Yet, it was quickly replaced by the child's playground, by the innocence, purity, and glorious naïveté of youth.

Could it be that THIS is what we're after?

Is it possible that it's not the wealth and the glitz and the gold and the glamour?

But a youthful, playful, outlook and perspective that turns our lives, our worlds, into a free-for-all playtime of happiness and innocent joy?

- **Possible:** shoot for the gold
- **Impossible:** know what either feels like (gold or plastic)
- **Repossible:** frolic in a bath of colorful plastic balls

5

PREPARE
THERE WILL BE DISBELIEF, JEALOUSY, AND ENVY

> "There is not a need to prove anything to anyone with your words. Let that which you—that which you are living—be your clear example to uplift others."
>
> — Esther Hicks

Whew, I feel like, here in book number ten in the Repossible series that I'm finally going to possibly put a stake in the ground or draw in the sand.

There will be some of you who might say something like:

> "Yeah, this is great for you, Mr. Charbonneau, but I really can't see myself living in this universe of enlightened play you supposedly life in."
>
> — Maybe You

What I'm of course shooting for here, rooting for in this book—in all of the Repossible books—is that you're here or almost here or will be here soon.

There's not a sign on the wall here in Playland that says:

Playland: Maximum Capacity 17

Or even 17,000 or 17,000,000.

Remember, quoting here from one of my not-really-fiction books, "Secret Bus to Paradise":

"It's not a physical place, on a map, or in a guidebook."

— Bradley Charbonneau, describing Paradise

It's a mindset and there's room for us all.

This chapter is called Prepare.

If you, my dearest reader, already here in book number ten, have ascended to a level anywhere near Play or at least a level above the lower levels way back at Ask or Dare, then there will be those who look at you with scorn, jealousy, and dare I say, hatred.

Maybe hatred is too strong.

What is that deep jealousy where people think something like:

"Why do they get that? I want what they have. It's not fair. I deserve it, too. Don't I?"

— Some People

Yet here you are in the book called Play where we're tossing around terms such as:

1. Enlightenment
2. Joy
3. Happiness
4. Lightness
5. Freedom
6. Smiling

7. Laughing
8. "Work at Play and Play at Work" (and understanding the difference)
9. Creativity
10. Purpose
11. Meaning
12. Childlike curiosity
13. Pleasure
14. Grin
15. Collaboration
16. Cooperation
17. Love

If someone recognizes one or two or all or any of these in you and they are not at this level, they might feel envious or jealous and they might show that in a negative or mean way.

I started out as a mathematics major in university. I still see things in line graphs, pie charts and numbers.

If you are living above the X-axis, the neutral, the regular, the normal, the expected, in a positive space and someone is below that line, down there in negativity and jealousy and want and longing and anger and maybe even hate, there's only one thing we can do.

Lift them up

OK, there are more options: ignore them, taunt them, etc. But that's not who we are.

Remember how people are allowed in the Playl conference hall? It was somewhere above 17,000,000, I think it was more like 17,000,000,000.

There's room for us all.

However.

In order to help those living at a lower level, vibrating at a lower frequency, we might need to reach our hand out to them, yes, down to them, and lift them up.

Do Not Descend

I feel like I don't give out too many "warnings." At least, I try not to.

But this one is important.

If you're living your life in a state of Play and someone else isn't quite there yet and they're going to bring you down, maybe even consciously trying to pull you down to where you are so they feel better about themselves or can stop being envious of you or whatever their reason, please be careful in not descending and staying there.

I see this all very visually. I hope I can relay what I see to you here.

While holding on to where you are, at the level on which you have ascended, the successful, joyful, fill-in-the-blank positive emotion that you've become accustomed to, reach down with your hand and pull them up.

Keep in mind that they might not actually want to come up. There are absolutely people who like complaining all the time, who enjoy putting other people down with degrading comments, and their personalities are intertwined with that behavior.

I don't know if they can be helped. It's really, really, really hard to help lift up people who don't want to be lifted up.

While we're on this topic, keep in mind that if they didn't ask for help, they also might not want—or need—it.

If you're floating on cloud nine and life is grand and you want to help your friends and family rise up to the level you're enjoying, they just not be all that interested.

Even if you go on and on about how wonderful your life has become, how joyful you feel, powerful, self-confident, full of purpose and happiness, they might be scared or incredulous or just not ready.

Not everyone will make it to book number ten in the Repossible series--even if we'd like them to, even if we want nothing more than to share the goodness we feel and have become in our hearts.

After two years of an international MBA program, I like to joke—although I'm not sure it's a joke—that the only thing I learned was from a Professor Inzirelli who told us, and I realize these aren't his own words:

"You can bring a horse to water but you can't make them drink."

— My MBA "Business Psychology" Professor

Whew, this has been a bit of a rough chapter.

Let's lighten things up on a higher note.

When you come across people who want to be helped, who are actively seeking to improve and might even ask you how you did it, how you're doing it, then life is grand, easy, and there are few things more delicious than reaching out your hand, offering them a step up, and saying to them: I'm rooting for you.

- **Possible:** descend to their level
- **Impossible:** descend and ascend
- **Repossible:** bring them up

6
PRACTICE
LIKE JUST ABOUT EVERYTHING, WE CAN GET BETTER AT PLAY

> "The imagination is a muscle. If it is not exercised, it atrophies."
>
> — Neil Gaiman

I'm going to keep the Neil Gaiman quote up there to begin this chapter but what if we just replaced "imagination" with Play?

> "Play is a muscle. If it is not exercised, it atrophies."
>
> — Bradley Charbonneau

I'm just going to go ahead and add my name to the new quote. Just like that.

I'm being playful, did you notice?

I'm not going to request a trademark for the phrase or ask permission if I can alter someone else's quote and make it for myself. I'm just going to do it.

There you have it: Play in Practice.

I'm practicing playing.

I took a quote and changed it and made it mine. Not a big deal, kind of fun, just goofing around here in this book.

Play isn't "a big deal" and I think that's part of the challenge many of us have with it.

Both of my kids play basketball. They also have math in school.

For neither of those things have they really grasped the concept of "practice makes perfect" (even though their writes chapter after chapter about it and even talks about it endlessly at the dinner table…).

The best part?

I've altered that quote too.

It's no longer "practice makes perfect," but:

 "Practice is Perfect."

— BRADLEY CHARBONNEAU

There I go again quoting myself! I wish you could see me now as I type this. I'm smiling. Writing this is fun for me. Whereas if people saw me they might think I'm working but I'm playing.

It's not getting to the NBA or reaching the bestseller list, it's about the practice.

We can practice play and, well, frankly, just as Mr. Gaiman started off this chapter, we have to practice playing or it will get rusty.

What's your version of Play you're going to practice? What's silly or maybe something others might take seriously (like writing the chapter of a book) that you make light of?

Head over to play-practice.repossible.com and share.

- **Possible:** wait until you're good at it
- **Impossible:** be an expert with zero experience
- **Repossible:** keep at it

PART II
L | LEAP

7

LOOSEN
WORK AT PLAY OR PLAY AT WORK

> "You cannot see the way out of a challenge if you are looking at it every day from the same level of mind, emotions, thoughts, and feelings of the past."
>
> — Dr. Joe Dispenza

It's a leap of faith. It's a loosening of pre-conceived definitions or understandings.

What if, just toy with me here for a minute, work didn't have to be all that we thought it was "supposed" to be?

What if we could:

1. Get the work done (like the boss asked)
2. Do an even better job
3. In less time
4. With more enjoyment
5. Come up with bigger and loftier ideas
6. While walking the dog (or on the beach or on a bike, etc.)
7. Call it "work" if anyone pressed us for what we were doing
8. Call it "play" because if we acknowledge that it's "play"

time instead of "work" time, our minds work more efficiently and effectively

See where I'm going? I could keep going.

Here is "Play at Work" in Real Life

I went to work on this chapter. I didn't sit at the computer. I didn't even turn on a laptop. I got the dog leash, rustled Pepper from his slumber, and went to play.

This is "work" (as most people know it) turned into "play" right before your eyes and you can see it all at play-loosen.repossible.com.

- **Possible:** Work at Play
- **Impossible:** neither
- **Repossible:** Play at Work

8

LOSE

NO WINNERS, NO LOSERS, NO SCORE

> "There is something at work that's bigger than us. It's about having a trust in life and being at peace that things are happening the way they should. You do what you do as well as you can do it, and then you don't worry or agonize about the outcome."
>
> — SHERILYN FENN

When I go into a meditation, or rather, let me rephrase, when I go into what turns out to be the good meditations, I don't have any expectations.

I'm not expecting a certain outcome, I'm not "keeping score," and I take from it what I get.

If I go into it an have a list of requirements and assumptions and even hopes then chances are good I won't get them.

As I dig deeper into this book called Play, I realize how much I reference the Meditate book.

Maybe it's because meditation is a form of play. It didn't used to be, I started meditating to "achieve" certain things (peace, health, etc.). Yep, I got those things. Yay!

But now that I'm, ahem, a more enlightened being, my goal for meditations is to have no goal.

Yep, it's hard.

Yes, it takes practice.

No, it doesn't always work.

But playing the game with no score, little-to-no expectations, and going for the pure game of it is the best way to play the game.

No score, no winner, no loser, just play over at play-ground. repossible.com.

- **Possible:** play to win
- **Impossible:** play to lose
- **Repossible:** don't keep score

9

LAUGH

RICH ROBINSON BRINGS STAND-UP TO CORPORATE

> "If I can get you to laugh with me, you like me better, which makes you more open to my ideas. And if I can persuade you to laugh at the particular point I make, by laughing at it you acknowledge its truth."
>
> — JOHN CLEESE

Rich Robinson is a professional speaker mostly for high-level corporate events in Asia.

Rich Robinson is a stand-up comedian.

He was backstage at an event in Singapore with 5 other speakers and he quickly learned that they had more experience than he did, owned a list of credentials longer than his, and were just plain more qualified than he was to speak on the topic of the conference.

Yet, somehow, Rich was the one they remembered.

Who remembered?

The audience.

Watch Bradley and Rich try to hold back (and fail) from telling at least one bad joke at play-rich.repossible.com.

- **Possible:** apologize for your humor
- **Impossible:** take everything seriously
- **Repossible:** make 'em laugh

10

LEONARD

"WORKING HARD" MIGHT TURN OUT BETTER IF YOU'RE "PLAYING LIGHTLY."

"The Universe is under no obligation to make sense to you."

— Neil deGrasse Tyson

Back in book #7, Meditate, we're "hard at work" sitting without a thought in our minds, cross-legged, and looking at flights to Tibet.

OK, sorry, none of that happened in the Meditate book.

Especially if you get to the book on Surrender where we let go of all of that "serious" stuff (e.g. cross-legged ...).

Which leads us to where we are now: Play.

Yep, I meditate every single morning.

Nope, I don't sit cross-legged and I don't need to move to Tibet.

But the absolute best meditations are the ones where I reach a level of Play that I previously only read about in books and heard stories about from "experienced gurus."

PRO TIP: We are all super. We are all natural. We are all supernatural. If I can do any of this stuff, so can you.

— The Management

Early on in my writing career, back when I "took it seriously" (READ: wasn't writing at all...), I would have never in a zillion years thought to share something in a book that is so personal, so "out there," so risky in the sense that you, dear reader, might think I've completely flown the coop and you would then toss this book into the nearest fireplace and get back to some good Wayne Dyer.

But that was then.

This is now.

This is Play.

We're having fun now.

I "don't care" anymore.

Well, that's not quite accurate. In some ways, I care much more than before, I care deeply.

What I don't care about is if you think I'm a nutcase.

What I do care about is sharing a crazy recap of a meditation as an invitation to go Play and try meditation and see where it takes you.

 OK, fine, you got me. The guy's name was Rupert. But there is no "R" in the word Play and I'm trying to stick to my section headings and chapter titles here!

— The (Lack of) Management

- **Possible:** meditate and play
- **Impossible:** keep it completely to yourself
- **Repossible:** dare to share a meditation recap in a book

I'm going to shed any and all sense of reality as I let you into the imagination, the dreams, the faraway places that meditation can take us, that surrounding to Play in our meditations, can take us.

All it takes is practice.

Don't say I didn't warn you.

Check out my rendezvous with Rupert at play-rupert.repossible.com.

11

LOUISE
THE RECESS LIFE

> "Recess is frivolous. We have to earn it. There are more productive things we could be doing. But I'd like to argue that we if we can incorporate recess and play into our life on a regular basis in everything we do, we actually will do everything else in life better."
>
> — Louise Wo

Louise Wo has a podcast called "The Recess Life."
Sure, you're in a book called Play. But she has a *podcast*, a *website*, a whole *purpose* based on the idea of Play.
How fun is that?
Could she be onto something?

> "We don't stop playing because we grow old; we grow old because we stop playing."
>
> — George Bernard Shaw

Just in case the word "recess" isn't ringing a bell for you, here are some definitions.

> **Recess:**
> *1. temporary withdrawal or cessation from the usual work or activity.*
> *2. a break between school classes (North America)*

Being from North America myself, I immediately go to that second definition: the school break. It's like brunch. It's after a period or two of classes and it's, at least in my rose-colored glasses memory, the best part of the school day.

Lunch is for eating lunch (and playing kickball) but recess? That was pure play. In fact, that's what you're *supposed to do*. You're sent outside to play.

Hello? Hello?

Why don't we do this as adults?

Yep, we eat lunch. I guess we take breaks. But sent outside to play?

Louise and I spend an entire podcast episode talking about the reasons she started the podcast, how play helps her in her daily life, how she organizes birthday parties, and then I even bring in words like...enlightenment.

"Ooh, gosh, enlightenment, it sounds so serious to me."

— Louise Wo

We bring our own experiences, our own words and definitions into the mix but at the end of the day, at the end of the episode, you'll have a better understanding of play and recess and how you can use it.

From the guy who dares write a "frivolous" book called Play to the woman who runs a podcast called "The Recess Life," I offer you our conversation.

It's a conversation we should be having on a regular basis.

Oh wait, that's exactly what Louise is doing.

Listen to our podcast episode over at play-louise.repossible.com.

- **Possible:** skip recess and stay in class
- **Impossible:** skip school except recess
- **Repossible:** It's recess!

PART III
A | ANCHOR

12

ANCHOR

EVEN THE SAILBOAT HAS AN ANCHOR

> "It is a far, far better thing to have a firm anchor in nonsense than to put out on the troubled seas of thought."
>
> — John Kenneth Galbraith

One of my favorite chapters of all of my books is called "The Cruise Ship & The Sailboat."

If we saw our own selves as giant cruise ships, we'd be difficult to steer, it can take quite a while to change course, but yet we're stable and going to crash through the biggest of waves.

One big challenge is we need to keep feeding it fuel—and it's a gas guzzler.

The sailboat on the other hand is agile, quick to change course, and is powered by the wind.

Sure, the wind can die down, but it will come back.

Yet a free sailing boat forever and ever can float away never to find land again.

Is it possible to be too free? Too flighty and light and happy?

There's a balance. For each of us it's different.

But even the sailboat has an anchor.
And just in case: a motor.

- **Possible:** anchor in the harbor and never sail
- **Impossible:** anchor in the open seas
- **Repossible:** sail the open seas and anchor in the harbor

13

ADWYNNA

IT STARTS WITH OPEN AND "UNCONSCIOUS COMPETENCE"

 "A life lived of choice is a life of conscious action. A life lived of chance is a life of unconscious creation."

— Neale Donald Walsch

If you give me a few minutes and I have your attention, I can explain what I mean by Play.

Here we are late in this book and, hopefully, you have an idea of what it is.

But just in case—and for my own understanding—it helps to "play" it out with someone, talk it though, not "work" at it, but just have a chat and try to explain what you mean.

Then what often happens is the person on the other end of the conversation explains it back to you in a way that you had never considered and in a way that makes more sense than anything you've ever tried.

Here's how this happened.

1. We planned to talk about Play.
2. We hit record.

3. We talked about lots of other, kind of related, stuff.
4. Then it happened.

For me, it was the clarity of the idea of "Four Stages of Competence." For Adwynna, or for someone else, it might have been something else.

But her mention of these stages, which I vaguely remember at some point in my life, really hit home in helping to understand and then further explain, in terms that are not just my own (e.g. enlightenment) that you might connect with even better.

From Wikipedia, here is the explanation of:

Four Stages of Competence

> *1. Unconscious Incompetence*
> *"The individual does not understand or know how to do something and does not necessarily recognize the deficit. They may deny the usefulness of the skill. The individual must recognize their own incompetence, and the value of the new skill, before moving on to the next stage. The length of time an individual spends in this stage depends on the strength of the stimulus to learn."*
>
> *2. Conscious Incompetence*
> *"Though the individual does not understand or know how to do something, they recognize the deficit, as well as the value of a new skill in addressing the deficit. The making of mistakes can be integral to the learning process at this stage."*
>
> *3. Conscious Competence*
> *"The individual understands or knows how to do something. However, demonstrating the skill or knowledge requires concentration. It may be broken down into steps, and there is heavy conscious involvement in executing the new skill."*

4. Unconscious Competence

"The individual has had so much practice with a skill that it has become "second nature" and can be performed easily. As a result, the skill can be performed while executing another task. The individual may be able to teach it to others, depending upon how and when it was learned."

From Wikipedia.

I'm an OK skier. It's sometimes fun. One of the biggest messages I'm shooting to get across in this book is the idea that we can turn many things, maybe not everything, into play.

For starters, here's a few huge ones in my own experience:

1. **Writing:** It used to be this "sacred" activity that I could only do when lightning struck and it was just the right time in autumn and ... yeah, that's why I didn't write much for a decade.
2. **Meditating:** I should move to Tibet, right? Wear the orange robe and eat mangoes for three years? Nope. How about sitting on a chair in my (locked) bathroom every single morning. Yep, that'll work.
3. **Skiing:** If I don't look at my feet, I follow the (better) skier in front of me, and just do what he or she does, it gets easier.

What's already at a level of Play for you? What can you do as "second nature" that's fun and easy and light?

What about something where you're not quite there yet? You'd like to be at a level of play but you can't seem to get there?

Below is a link to our video and below that is a comment section (after you click the link). Share where you're in Play mode and what is next to bring into your Play arena.

- **Possible:** Conscious Competence

- **Impossible:** Staying at the Top of the Mountain
- **Repossible:** Unconscious Competence

Highlights of our conversation where we were "playing" to the point of pulling out nuggets of wisdom like this chapter are to be seen in their full and "this was supposed to be a regular Zoom call" glory at play-adwynna.repossible.com.

PART IV
Y | YIELD

14

YELL

SCREAM FROM THE MOUNTAINTOPS

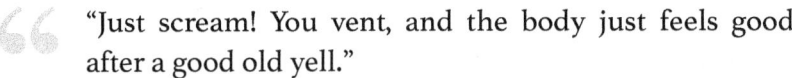 "Just scream! You vent, and the body just feels good after a good old yell."

— CAROL BURNETT

I was probably a mechanic in a past life because I think often in terms of input and output, like gasoline and exhaust with a car engine.

I'm not a big yeller or screamer. I'm more impressed with the school teacher who can calm down a middle school class with silence and patience rather than screaming and yelling.

Yet, there is a place for screaming and yelling.

Have you ever been so mad, frustrated, angry, betrayed that you're yelling at the top of your lungs, maybe tears rolling down your cheeks as your blood boils and you finally get out of breath from the sheer physical exhaustion of screaming?

Or when you're so sad, sobbing, messy, snotty-nose sad where you're uncontrollably letting it all out?

Then, sometimes, that anger or that sadness turns into a smile.

That might lead to a chuckle, a giggle, then it occasionally goes all the way to a laugh.

The "uncontrollable" part of those emotions seem to somehow go from one extreme to the other and yet they're so close to each other.

Often the transition comes from an external factor. Ideally, someone who pulls you across the river to go from the anger or sadness and right into the neighborhood of joy or even giddy silliness.

How can those two extremes be so close together?

What if the extremes weren't so much on the opposite sides of each other but more both out at the end of a long road and then they are just a slightly different flavor or direction of the same thing?

They're both extreme emotions. They're both actions we don't have, at least hopefully, all that often.

Yet they can be almost interchanged.

Don't get me wrong. If your dog dies, I'm not saying you're going to turn on a dime and laugh about it.

But once we're over the initial shock of the external factor, it's up to us as to how we further deal with it.

Anger, sadness, and play are not that far from each other.

They're all out on the limb pretty far and it's almost as if you're out that far already all you have to do to go from one to another is a slight shift in how you see it.

Ready for an oddball challenge?

The next time you're out in the woods or on an empty beach or maybe it's in your car on the highway, scream with anger about something you're not happy about.

Just whatever comes to mind.

Really let it go, let it out, let yourself roar with anger or sadness.

For me, I would yell at cancer. It took both my mom and dad earlier than I would have liked.

It shouldn't take long. Screaming with anger is tiring. If you feel the tide turning towards laughter or any kind of joy or happiness or lightness, go with it.

If the anger or sadness keep coming, go with it.

If the joy doesn't come, force it.
Then roll with it.
Remember, these emotions are close cousins. They'll meet up out there if you set up the meeting.

- **Possible:** scream until you're hoarse
- **Impossible:** hold it all in all the time
- **Repossible:** yell until you get it out

15

YODEL
IT'S NOT FOR EVERYONE

 "This is my last chip."

— Tom Charbonneau

My dad probably never would have yodeled.
I know it's an odd word. For clarification, here's the definition:

> **yodel:** *"to sing with frequent changes from the ordinary voice to falsetto and back again, in the manner of Swiss and Tyrolean mountaineers."*

I bring my dad into this chapter because he wasn't the playful type that I am portraying in this book.

My uncle Wayne would have yodeled.

My mom would have yodeled.

But not my dad.

I add this chapter to make sure you don't think that Play is only fun and funny, silly and slapstick, or even only enlightened and floating.

My dad *thought* he was pretty funny. He had jokes sometimes where you weren't sure if the punchline already came through. Then you felt bad because you missed it.

But you felt even worse when he had to then explain it all and it still wasn't funny.

But he had his moments of Play.

One of his favorite tricks was, while at a Mexican restaurant, sitting at the table with the endless baskets of fresh tortilla chips, he would proudly announce:

"This is my last chip."

— Dad

But then what he did next was the funny part.

I could tell you the story here but it's better live so I'm going to share quite a private video with you here of part of my speech at his memorial service.

It's 5 minutes and a tribute not to the yodeling type of Play but to the witty, the charming, and the loved ones who did manage to get in some Play just when you thought they were all business. Watch the 5-minute clip at play-tom.repossible.com.

- **Possible:** eat all of the chips
- **Impossible:** don't eat any chips
- **Repossible:** save one chip for last while you enjoy the rest of the basket

16

YIELD
CHISEL AWAY TO FIND WHAT'S UNDERNEATH

 "There's a sculpture inside that block of granite I need to set free."

— Some Artist Probably Said

Here we are at the end of this book and I'm going to deliver a whopper of an idea.

Maybe I should have set this up in the beginning but I'm not sure you would have "believed" me. In fact, I'm not sure you'll "believe" me now.

It's of course, just my opinion.

I believe we all have Play in us.

There you go. That's it. That's my big revelation.

The quote at the opening of this chapter is based on something I heard at some point along the way and it's about the artist who "sees" the sculpture inside of the block of granite (or wood or clay).

I used to not really get this or even believe it.

Now that I've written 27 books, I get it.

I start with a blank page and it comes to me.

The sculptor takes a chisel (or whatever it is that sculptors use) and starts *freeing* the sculpture that's *trapped* inside.

In fact, it's the artist's duty to free what's inside. Maybe the artist is the one person who sees that particular sculpture inside and he or she will make sure it is set loose.

Can you see this with me here?

The thing is, I believe we are all those blocks of granite. We all have something inside of us, we all have Play in us, that just needs to be set free.

It's in there.

Of that I am sure.

It's just whether or not a sculptor comes along and chisels away the heavy stone surrounding it, practically suffocating it, to let it live.

We all have Play in us.

Who has the chisel?

- **Possible:** see the finished product (sculpture) after the artist chiseled away everything else
- **Impossible:** see only a block of granite
- **Repossible:** chisel away to discover what's underneath

AFTERWORD

I continue to struggle writing this book because I think back to my life on October 31, 2012, the day before I started writing every single day.

I say I struggle because had I read this book called Play, I would have scoffed, shrugged, and probably tossed it in the garbage.

Because at *that* point in my life, I couldn't imagine such a level of being, such a lightness in my step, such a joy in my heart.

Yet here I am, eight years later, and most of my life is play.

Am I drowning in buckets of cash flowing from the skies?

Nope.

Is it that I'm overwhelmed from the fame and the endless calls to have me perform on stage?

Ugh uh.

Oh, I know, is it that I'm tired of the celebrities begging me to share the spotlight?

Not exactly.

Maybe it's a profound a sense of purpose the fills my heart on a daily basis, a practice that doesn't make me perfect but a practice that is perfect, a joy in the tiniest of wins and a chuckle at the biggest of failures, a skip in my step, a wink to those in the know, and the butterflies of the unknown who flitter in my stomach?

Yes.

I used to be there.

Now I'm here.

My wish, my dream, is that you are on the path, that you have one foot, even a toe, even your pinky toe, on the path.

Because I know as much as I know anything, that once you have a taste of Play, you can never undo it and you'll never want to.

EPILOGUE

As with most of my books, I'm going to keep working on them. The upside (well, and the downside...) of an artist's work is that it's never finished.

If you haven't already, come on over to play.repossible.com and join in the game.

It will continue to grow, evolve, and, with you there, it will become a part of you.

I'm going to sign this from a future time and place.

Ready?

Bradley Charbonneau
In-Person "Repossible Retreat"
Bali, Indonesia
2022

ACKNOWLEDGMENTS

Early on in my life, my dad told me, in so many words and with lots of other words and lessons in between:

 "Work hard, study, learn, teach."

— Dad

From my mom, I'm paraphrasing from an entire lifetime, it pretty much boiled down to this one word.

It's not really going to come as a big surprise.

 "Play."

— Mom

ABOUT THE AUTHOR

I just edited this "About the Author" page and I added at the bottom, "This is my twenty-seventh book."

I don't know about you, but I can't imagine doing anything 27 times that didn't involve lightness, joy, and *play*.

I mean, sure, brushing your teeth, paying taxes every year (for 27 years), fine, yes.

But these have been 27 *voluntary actions* on my part. They're books, not socks, they take time, care, love, effort, passion, time, sweat, tears (sadness and joy), and I can't imagine doing them without an element of **Play**.

I'm not an author because of the millions in annual royalties (not yet) or the glorious fame (is this coming at some point?) or the ... OK, you get the idea.

I'm an author mostly because:

1. I can't not be. It's who I am.
2. I have a message to share, a voice to be heard, a story to tell.
3. It's Play.

Sometimes, I struggle with the idea that Play is reserved for the elite, the enlightened, or that you can only play IF you are enlightened.

As if there's an order to it:

1. Enlightenment
2. Play

My wife and I traveled through Eastern Africa. Especially clear in my memory is a country called Malawi where so many little boys played with a stick and the tire of a bicycle. They would, with great accuracy, push the stick into the inside of the tire and run with it and the tire would roll.

They laughed so much. They giggled. They created their own world. They had "nothing" yet maybe they had "everything."

Maybe I have the ordering wrong. Maybe it's like this:

1. Play
2. Enlightenment

Maybe we need to adopt the Play mindset before we reach enlightenment.

Those boys aren't waiting around for enlightenment (or whatever their version of that is). Of course, yes, they're kids and kids already have Play built into their daily lives.

But when we bring this to adults, when we come back home and think of this in our own regular daily lives, can we also turn around the order of things?

Can we first *Play* and then *Enlighten*?

I'm not waiting around to find out.

This book is called Play.

You might notice I don't have a book called Enlighten.

Yet.

So far, Play is working out just fine.

Oh so fine.

I currently live in a little town outside of Utrecht in The Netherlands with my wife Saskia, famous two young boys of "The Adventures of Li & Lu" fame, and our at-least-as-famous dog, Pepper.

This is my twenty-seventh book.

It is far, far, far from my last.

Find, ask, discuss, play, and dare at:
bradleycharbonneau.com

facebook.com/bradley.charbonneau.author
twitter.com/brathocha
instagram.com/brathocha

ALSO BY BRADLEY CHARBONNEAU

Most of my books are also available as audiobooks (which I giddily narrate). Search for my name at your favorite audiobook distributor, slip on your headphones, and let me take you away.

Repossible

Repossible

Every Single Day (+ Playbook)

Ask

Dare

Create

Decide

Meditate

Spark

Surrender

Play

Celebrate

Evaluate

Elevate

Frequency

Every Single Day

Every Single Day Playbook

Every Single Day Kids

Every Single Day Teens (I want to write this one because I want to read this one...)

Every Single Day Parents

Charlie Holiday

Now Is Your Chance (1)

Second Chance (2)

Chance of a Lifetime (3)

For Creatives

Audio for Authors

Meditation for Creatives (2020)

Shorts

Secret Bus to Paradise

Where I (Already) Am

Pass the Sour Cream

A Trip to Hel

Drive-By Dropping

Li & Lu

The Secret of Kite Hill (1)

The Secret of Markree Castle (2)

The Key to Markree Castle (3)

The Gift of Markree Castle (4)

Driehoek (5)

Really Old ...

urban travel guide SAN FRANCISCO

THE END

I t's time to play.

www.ingramcontent.com/pod-product-compliance
Lightning Source LLC
Chambersburg PA
CBHW071315040426
42444CB00009B/2025